# She Was So Naked

Lourdes Vázquez

Translation by
Enriqueta Carrington

PREMONITION

2015

Front cover photo: © *Espiga de arroz* by Rafael Rosario Laguna
Cover and interior design: Margarita Maldonado Colón
ISBN: 10-069235297X

## Acknowledgments

Some of these poems were originally published in Spanish in *Un enigma esas muñecas* (Madrid: Torremozas, 2015)-Honorary Mention, Paz Price 2014. The poem *I Like Stories With Bitches As Characters* first appeared in *The Gathering of the Tribes*.

*Gracias mil*, many thanks to Loretta Collins Klobah for the final revision of this manuscript.

*She Was So Naked*

# CONTENTS

# I

*Elle était fort déshabillée*
-Première Soirée, Rimbaud.

# Were You Sleeping?

*I* had just met you,
  I stripped myself of protocols
and invited you to hold you close.
That winter night
I wanted to ask you for the meaning
of your moans, for the frown of sorrow
shaped on the skin of your brow.
Because despite our holding each other
like two handfuls of water
joined in a storm
your soul flowed unchecked
as if all its yearnings
and futures were glued
to the secrets of the abyss.


Certainly you were asleep and time,
                    slowly, very slowly,
became ingrained in that room.
I only sat on the edge of the bed
facing the wide window
to allow the passing of my sadness
at having known you so closely.

# Edison, NJ

*I* live very close to India. I take
the train and a route of waters and
railroads brings me near a temple
with three oblong domes facing
East: as ancient scriptures
ordain. Behind its wooden
doors, adorned with sacred
fauna and flora, parishioners
surrender themselves, offering
profound fervor to the
divinity in blue porcelain.

I live so close I can hear
the strange signs of peace they
profess to each other and smell
spices and oils on the altars. I can
see the goddess Lakshmi in her red sari
accompanied by two white elephants,
or Saraswati— goddess of diamond-bright rivers —.
Both of them incrusted into a poster in Edison
Station announcing: 'The 6 top Indian channels'.
It's curious to see goddess Devi pronounce in favor of
the Kadambari clothing store: "A Fashion Lover."

The Ganges in the distance, that
is not clay, not swamp,
not excrement, only toxin.

# The Broom

*T*oday I looked for you in that other,
  kid like you,
like you, she had a baby,
great dark eyes and elongated face.
I curbed my impulses to caress you,
but that other and her politics of death restrained me.

With my breast compressed
and a window open to all
the dark foam of sorrow
I walked back.
It's just that I had not noticed
How martyrdom perfumes
with gladioli the stones along the way.

Suddenly I no longer looked for your face,
but mine: to take care
and protect myself against so much destruction,
which acts like a simple flu-—
it suddenly strikes out with its great hand,
and you end up surrounded by cameras
or by the side of a zebra crossing;
to gather you up again
among the leaves of the little plants I grow
so I can realize how so much death
is now to be found next to the broom that cleans my floor.

# The Small Amount Of Energy

*i*s used in giving explanations.
To everybody:
because I have not been there,
have not arrived, have not shown up.

What can I say?

–It has not been possible for me–.

I explain I have not been able.
I insist I have found it hard.

And so with time I've become a parrot
trained to speak precise phrases. An oven
with controlled temperature.

I keep justifying myself to those
who don't deserve it,
who don't deduce,
don't understand.

It's to myself I owe explanations.
I must make it clear how much it has cost me
to move with grace, among stones
and crags and in the middle of the raging sea,
while I hold up my entrails and comb this tangled hair.

# Watch That Image

*T*he TV shot out images of women
with multiple petticoats in white
cheering the great sea. One of them
slipped into the subway at the very
instant when I left for work.

Vigorous breasts, impertinent waist,
innumerable embroidered pleats
and ribbons in white, because I love you in white.
The lullaby of that machine opened its pores
to receive the ample petticoat on its seats.
I did not suspect.

At night I picked up a random book
and on its jacket a skirt rested
on the hump of a sewing machine
like the intact ruin of the day.
Nor did I investigate.

# City, I Sleep Alone

*i* look forward to snoring by the side of a man
   who squats and is painted blue.
His tongue comes near my body
like a butterfly                    amidst snow.
I ask you that my referent
to this
theater of
death
may contain clear water
for the fountains
and that his technicolor tongue
may be forerunner to all the tenderness of a man in love.

# Paris Fetish

*E*s *un viaje along the streets of Paris.*
They swing among flea markets and
lakes that indicate dark wisdoms. A bird
made of light is balanced in the air by
means of a fishing pole,

an elongated fountain with designs of
Greek columns contains waters as silvery
as the thousand moons of this planet.
A little lamb, magical and soft—like all
lambs that exist in dreams—allows itself
to be caressed.

A gray-haired elf with a small body adores
my body, producing a little transparent
receptacle with vin rosé.

How to explain that my liquids were
released, that is to say: all the fluids
contained and I felt audacious, weightless,
transparent.

# Orishas

*I* look out of the window in the first light of day.
It's my routine.
I look out of the window to be sure
dawn contains golden
and more golden rays, that is to say golden.
Gold and gold and oranges and more goldens,
destroying the gray left behind by night.
It's the moment when in damp
pampas the green of grass reappears,
the dunes of Maranhão
turn into diamonds,
water is already translucent in Titicaca Lake,
and palm trees give thanks for fire on my island,
making their fronds dance in unison.
Then shamans open up space
with the intense music of drums,
so that people like me can begin
the work of Orishas. That's when I give myself
permission
to build the agenda of the day.
I close the window and prepare coffee.

# It's Not Enough

*J*ust to purchase
a couple of red leather suitcases
at some exotic store in the South.
It's not enough to lock myself in there
so that I can be tossed out at some
railway station or into some cranny
of an obscure airport, and have someone
pick us up, me and my scared little heart.

It's not enough. Because life is
more complicated,
circumstances more abstruse,
daily life more agile,
existence more pleasant,
fuller of dancing giraffes,
of grains of rice and milk,
of weeping and laughter,
wider than the waves,
higher than the whale's flight,
more sublime than the laughter of children.

# Chimaera

If I chop a couple of tomatoes
   and arrange them to the left
of the rice. If I multiply them
as in the story of the bread and wine;
that is to say: if I continue to chop
tomatoes and set them out
to the left of the rice for my friends —and
                    neighbors— I must add.

This whole apocryphal and sensual
ceremony of blood-stained,
vegetable red,
the swollen brown
of rice grains,
is almost a chimaera.
I don't imagine myself
distributing so much lust.

# The Image Of A Crow

*i* often see entering
and exiting my surroundings.

At dawn he approaches,
extends his little black hat and
greets me with a good day.
The seduction begins here.
He shows his teeth—
Master crow—
creating a language
almost impossible to understand.
I try to be cordial.
I discreetly return his greeting
and act as if I were listening,
as if I paid attention to his dialogue,
but the real truth is I go
along observing Master crow
with great caution.
His threadbare garments.
His opaque teeth and hat.
The bad smell of his plumage.
Not to mention his flight.
Not ethereal at all.

# Earthquakes Were Triggered

*W*hen she discovered it was not
    she, but the surroundings. That she
remained intact and unconditional.
More luminous every day,
with a special splendor flowing
from her skin and eyes.

Now a smile of peace and yearning
for better things comes to rest
on her fortitude. She does not recall opacity.
Only the way clouds clear.

Because and suddenly cosmovision
does not matter, it's the crystalline silhouette,
the touch of porcelain, the sea-star
smile that entertain her.

Because she was fed up with collaborating
for discontent, it's the lion who
upholds her: his forceful mane,
the great crystal teeth.

Because in the neck of that labyrinth
only storms circulate around
the battered avenger, the sick recluse
and the neighbor woman with the spotless
swimming pool she cannot use.

Because these small deaths are
like scratches in sphinxes' eyes.
Warranties of oblivion.

# Mourning

*W*hen I learned about the death of the little boy in Tanzania,
that little boy with a smile like delicate tasty milk,
when I knew he was gone to play with Persephone's
seeds, I made myself burn aromatic herbs with
the stone liquor distilled in those lands
and his small ring-finger, cracked and black.

Because the dead child needs a journey that's crystalline
and free of digressions, from the hand of expansive
and generous  powers. With rites, herbs and grains and Ochún
with her long starched skirt, in the sweet wide lake
beweeping the catastrophe.

Aromas and balsams for the mother, out of her wits,
tisane of mercury for the tearful father,
cloud or charmed soot to prevent cruelty,
mouthful of the powerful elixir for the surrounding
forms, smoke bath for sleeplessness and the
invocation to sleep.

Because someone said:
"there is no love, only small tests of love."

# I Believe

*E*ach of my particles
is scorching in the heat of the fire.
I'm not dreaming.
I only describe the event just as it is.
I disappear into a thousand fragments
and become a fraction of shadow.
I'm not crazy either.
I only speak the experience
even if it sounds suspicious.

I believe it's necessary that
my innards be shaken up,
renewing the trunk that upholds this building,
as a reptile replaces its
garments and the woman at that corner
barters youngsters with very white
and scented sexes.

# The Possible

*T*he few times I've seen her she's silent.
Or rather, she's found without
voice or movement of her body.
Something is broken in there:
neurons that no longer work,
nonexistent enzymes.

Something is broken, I've said already,
with the exception of her gaze.

There are no sparks of melancholy,
nor can one glimpse compassionate or loving signs.
Only the concrete perception of
a bony and wrathful old woman

I relive the life we had together,
when we imagined the possible.

# I Continue On A Journey

Side by side with protective
  people who save me from great emotions.
They repair the car I travel in
and keep me company through rocky
regions and spotless cities.
Sometimes they give me an elixir of life to drink,
or point out a perfect drink:
"Coffee with milk and milk-skin."  Milk-skin?
What a detail!
They invite me to that table that I
may savor fresh papayas and oranges
in season.

I invoke the warmth and roundness
of this tenderness, the open backbone of memory,
the dark aroma of the wound.

They also dress me in fabrics of delicate
cotton and brilliant colors and point out to me
the coffers that contain tens of gems,
onyx and water in transparent cups.
Water that becomes extensive kisses
under an ausubo tree.

Ausubo tree turned into fountain.
Fountain hidden in your fruit.

# Do You See?

*I*t's the garden, quivering with waters, grounds, stems, and buds: significant oxygens serving the master's pleasure. The magnificent temperature and the murmur of human voices evince the astounding beauty of the roses. It induces a sort of waking sleep. The garden allows us to yearn for it. One perceives, on that side, a fountain with goldfish, hyacinths overflowing with health, and a minimal labyrinth made of paving stones.

Protection and defense. Recent residue of the age of fires. To find the way back it's advisable to relinquish the thread of the skein.

To this garden, which I describe as rectangular and surrounded by brick walls, a treasure has been added. A few of the chosen are generous with the secret. It's a curious opening in the ground where great seas flow together, cradling the marvelous creatures of a mythical island. Propitious site of flavors that tempt pilgrims and tourists from the North to venerate the great phosphorescence.

Let's go in.

# We Conceived You

We conceived you in a field guarded
by the Devas of a great mountain
and the green of a hemisphere
that sustains life like a powerful soldier.

On the banks of that stream,
healthful and brilliant,
we exchanged fluids,
penetrating each other's aura
like invincible and merry shamans.

Your father and I thought you up,
even if he does not remember.

# No Return

*T*here are days when she overflows her banks.
In a hurry, she keeps busy.
She goes out to the store, buys
and organizes spices and foods
by size, texture, and color.
She prepares an exotic menu and throws herself
into the street once again.
She buys a blouse,
two lipsticks,
she holds conversations with everybody she meets.
She returns home, takes a bath with salts, oils, and foams.

Now the mirror, the creams and powders for the skin,
all of her dedicated to herself,
desperately occupied
by so much to do.

And so her days go by,
pushing at subtle darkness,
the delicate shadow in the air,
the murky noise of silence.
The secret that devours
a couple when there is no return.

# Hope

*T*here, where moon-rays and wind-howl
  stretch out,
I declared my love to you.
There was hardly time—
it was all so rushed.
Between astonishment and joy,
we seemed like beginners
dealing with intimacies under an
almond tree, hiding
from grown-ups:  with all the uproar
of the shy embrace, like that of teenagers with
pimply faces.

I would have liked
to remain in the hollow
of your breast for a long spell,
perhaps the whole autumn. Let
the leaves cover our lips,
and cold protect this tenderness,
so that we could recover the memory
of those who are in love and at ease;
not like an event that can
be written in some encyclopedia,
but with the expectation of one who yearns
for a new eclipse. To the beat of a heart
with a bleeding gaze: between the confused triumph
of the moment and the hope that there would be no good-byes.

# The Apple

*B*ehold, I offer you
Gala's fruit
—my man—

that she may be the Muse
to attend your sorrows
or insecurities. Behold, I can
part with the cluster of apples
—my little girl. Behold, I devise

a mask with the fruit's
peel for the princess disfigured
in the operating room. Behold,
I can disguise the seed with cyanide
—that transparent, flavorless substance—

and lean in through the scientist's laboratory
window and seduce him into chewing it.

Because one must not trust in apple trees,
they have their fashions and tastes, moving
around at night, roots and all, to modify
surroundings. Nor should one trust in their fruits,
they have ingenuity to alter texture, color, and aroma
with the only goal of setting goddesses' dreams
aflame.

# Sign or Signal

The language he knows is
an imaginary one, a temple
with music in a dream country,
an old man whistling and celebrating
by the side of his housewife who feeds
the heart a tisane of gleaming
good wine with a flowery bouquet.

But like all tortuous
roads of love, a dove
carrying substances, secretions,
vibrations and affections shoots out
from my altar.

Sign or signal he suckled
from his mother: mental correspondent
in the soul.

Sign or signal he receives
and emits in quantity or degree
and with alternate goals.

Sign greater than the shiniest
mirror in the world.

Exotic vehicle that guesses
the flirting or perversion
of an Oedipus Rex investigating
the death of the father:
that mangled monarch
who still evokes settlements of sorrow.

# Facing The Façade

*F*acing the façade of that restaurant
   the menu invites me to sit down alone.
Because I am a free woman, not accountable
to anybody.

—How well one hears you! —I told myself.

I saw myself fold the napkin on my lap,
savored the hot jasmine tea,
The waiter who served us one day
tossed a smile at me and
I realized I was surrounded by couples.
A stab of anguish skewered my heart.

—Oh my life, how I bleed!

I ran to look for you.

# Wind, You

*Wind, you who set
hope free.*
—Clemente Soto Vélez

*I*sland.
   There exists an island where turtle-doves nest
and the old walk with a light step
to early-morning mass.
Algae have arrived at the shore,
children toy with the singular peace of the day
and the banana grove rises straight as a flowering penis.

A couple seated on the stairs of the church
waits for the sun to slap them,
a girl gives out bread crumbs
to the pigeons in the public square,
and I ask permission to touch your skin, black
as my clay vessel,       your eyes,
transparent as the bottom of a virgin sea.


Island.
Imaginary line at the center of the globe:
         *Wind, you.*
Point in the darkness of the ocean.
Dream of dead twins.
A suspicion.

# Alphabet

*T*hree letters admiring a sunset.
The first one slithers or coils like
a trained snake.
The second is a false step-stool
with three rungs
            (that strange number
again).

The third letter is a crossedroad
where a meeting
is proposed at the very center
of the sphere.

Three—it indicates Cabbala
with its significants—its
equivalent to understanding.

To explain my meaning:   *SEX.*

# Wonder Woman

*A*midst the Hudson's vegetable music,
cross-barred by mangrove swamps,
the train is outlined along the liquid width.

Head spins,
heart accelerates,
memory is interrupted.

Wonder Woman
knows a magical entrance
to my enemy's world.

Tongue parched and slit in two.
Gutted and exhausted
my enemy emerges from
the junctures of the morning
persecuting everything I am:
this house,
the cat,
the bad breath in my sickbed.

Something more I must say:
the water shapes
indecipherable animals, moths,
and great secret hollows.

# A Stroll

...to Elsa Noya for the lovely
stroll around La Recoleta...

*O*n that horizon, the nymph takes care
of the cemetery with its small alleys
and lanterns, as if the dead
could understand strolling and gossiping.

She is the nymph who proclaims the delights
of the forest. The forest, I've said,
with its green and greener bifurcations
and tens of songbirds feeding
in tree canopies.

Over there one glimpses a couple, arguing
heatedly about G. knows what. A few people
walk beyond the railing while we
go entering the darkness of the grove,
discovering its breadth, the thickness and density
of its vegetation, its specimens, the inches of annual rainfall,
and the ring where tens
of creatures dance around the fountain,
that which one cannot forget.

Shall we go on?

# Without Memory Or Oblivion

*Elle était fort déshabillée*
—Rimbaud

*H*er arms remained there, where they'd
been thrown. Her head, belly, navel,
those ears of hers, all of her like a calf
in sacrifice, her spirit mashed against
that fence and the fluids of her body
paralyzed, like songbirds sunk in sewage.

For all purposes *il corpo in letargo* in
the middle of the road, despoiled of
her dignity, her decorum torn away, a
thousand times broken, thrown into
emptiness, fallen to the earth and thrown
again. Never to get up and to stay, a
rotting carcass with roaches and little
mice eating your pieces.

Nobody leans out to see. Nobody. Until
it's too late and the decomposition of your
body makes paramedics and policemen
run away.

To die on the highway must be more
brutal than to die sprawled on the floor
of your room like the Finnish woman who
dreams of winter fires. To die burst apart
by tires, by the weight of the machine, the
little fragments of metal digging into you,
because your head exploded, madam; and
the kidneys jumped like defective bells
and the belly was left rotten by flies, the
way we blacks die, without memory or
oblivion.

# II

*Considera, alma mía, esta textura*
*áspera al tacto, a la que llaman vida…*
-Dos meditaciones, Rosario Castellanos

# I Like Stories With Bitches As Characters

↓

*T*rue bitches:  the one who desires her
progeny the one who abandons it
the one who guards it jealously
the one who despises it
the one who kills the puppies
the pack of mongrel bitches
who wander around my mother's
neighborhood without anything
being done about it
howling +bloody+
destroying their pieces
for the sake of carnal odors,
of she-animal fights. ↓
My sister and her love for bitches.
My father declaring his yard a burial
ground for bitches. ↓

→→ My neighbor's dog, small, white, furry.
She carries her around in her purse with
the  little dancing head looking out at
everybody in the train which she has taken
at West 4th station. People smile when
they see the little furry one. At 14th Street
a cop pushes through. He tries to board
the train in the middle of the crowd and
PAFFFFFF! the cudgel sets loose and
whacks the animal. Has anything been left
of the poor thing? ↓
↓↓
→ The islands of Sicily and Tortola have the
same climate. Everything that grows in

Sicily grows in Tortola. I have lived on both
islands and when I would finish a poem
such as this one, I'd put it into an envelope
and give it to any fisherman who was
about to go out to high sea. Fishermen
always travel to larger lands to sell their
catch. The fishermen give the envelope to
a pilot and the pilot delivers it at the other
side of the sea, to be published and read.
We've seen so many bitches on these
islands. They arrive with the fishermen,
pups and old ones + they go off to the
mangrove swamps and the hills where
they reproduce, feeding on everything
that moves around them.

→ Dog = "mammal, carnivorous,
domestic, of very variable size, shape and
fur according to the breed. A sharp sense
of smell and some intelligence. Profoundly
loyal." = Reads the dictionary.
↓
↓
Dulce,
That freckled bitch.
WAS HOT!!!
Was hot!!!

→ → That is to say, all the males went
after her. One night four dogs ambushed
her. We tried to get the males off her. How?
One throws boiling water at the male's
member. Note that the member is red,
burning with blood. One strikes the male's
back with a cane as many times as may be
necessary. One must strike hard, until the
pain in the bones is stronger than lust. ↓

→I've never had Dulce's good fortune, or rather that intensity and I don't know whether these days I love Dulce or I hate her.

↓

↓A bitch was watching Mariana hemming the puertorriqueña flag. Mariana was sitting in a soft easy chair. Two cushions against the back-rest. The easy chair was placed in front of her window, over there in the Bronx, to be precise. It was winter and Mariana preferred natural light to yellow irregular candlelight, that's why she was in front of that window.→ →

↓Here is Mariana hemming our flag. The black, golden-spotted bitch climbed onto the windowsill. Mariana has decided to open the window. —Get outta here, you're blocking my view!

Voilà!!!

The bitch was frightened; she took a false step, plunging down five stories. She's fallen with a wallop on the sidewalk, her skull opened in a thousand smithereens. A woman in scanty clothing, her blouse loaded with brooches, hoops in her earlobes, gold bracelets + rings, stopped beside the corpse only for a few moments and went on her way.

2006

**Lourdes Vázquez** is a well-known poet and writer from Puerto Rico living in the USA. Her work had appeared in numerous anthologies and journals and besides English had been translated to Italian, French, Swedish, and Portuguese. Among the latest *Appunti dalla Terra Frammentata* (Italia: EDIBOM Edizione Letterarie, 2012), a poetry anthology in Italian and *Un enigma: esas muñecas* (Madrid: Torremozas, *2015)*, Honorable Mention 2014 Paz Prize for Poetry (USA)

**Enriqueta Carrington** is a NEA Literary Translation Recipient 2015. She is the translator of several volumes of poetry, including *Treasury of Mexican Love Poems* (Hippocrene Books, Treasury of Love Series) and *Samandar: Libro de Viajes/Book of Travels* by Lourdes Vázquez (Argentina: Editorial Tsé-Tsé, 2007). She holds a Ph.D. in mathematics from Rutgers University, and taught for many years at the National University of Mexico, the University of California at Berkeley, Temple University, and Rutgers University.

www.ingramcontent.com/pod-product-compliance
Lightning Source LLC
Chambersburg PA
CBHW041806040426
42448CB00005B/294